A Different Way Home

A play

Jimmie Chinn

Samuel French — London
New York - Toronto - Hollywood

Please see page iv for further copyright information

FIRST PRODUCTION

Leslie was first performed by **Antony Linford** at The Duke's Head, Richmond, Surrey, in December 1986. The play was directed by the author.

It was broadcast on BBC Radio Four on Wednesday July 13th, 1988, with **Bernard Cribbins** playing Leslie. Gerry Jones directed.

The two plays, *Leslie* and *Maureen*, under the collective title of *A Different Way Home* were first presented together at the Coliseum Theatre, Oldham, on January 30th 1998.

Roy Barraclough played both parts.

Directed by **Kenneth Alan Taylor**
Designed by **Celia Perkins**
Lighting designed by **Jezz Hellins**
Sound by **Julie Washington**

PRODUCTION NOTES

These two plays can be presented separately or together to form a complete play in two acts.

In the production at the Coliseum Theatre, Oldham, directed by Kenneth Alan Taylor, both parts were played by a single actor, Roy Barraclough. However, the parts can obviously be played by a man and a woman.

The setting is the same for both plays (acts) and can be as simple or as elaborate as circumstances permit. At Oldham, the designer, Celia Perkins, provided a very detailed setting of both Leslie's living-room and kitchen, allowing both characters to move freely between the two rooms.

Act I (*Leslie*) runs for approx. 55 minutes and Act II (*Maureen*) approx. 35 minutes.

J.C.

Other plays by Jimmie Chinn published by
Samuel French Ltd

After September
Albert Make Us Laugh
But Yesterday (one-act)
From Here to the Library (one-act)
Home Before Dark, *or*, **The Saga of Miss Edie Hill**
In By the Half (one-act)
In Room Five Hundred and Four (one-act)
Interior Designs (one-act)
Pity About Kitty (one-act)
A Respectable Funeral (one-act)
Something to Remember You By
Straight and Narrow
Sylvia's Wedding
Take Away the Lady
Too Long an Autumn (one-act)

To Roy—with deepest gratitude and, of course,
in memory of Edie.

Jimmie Chinn

ACT I

A room in Lancashire

Leslie enters in overcoat and scarf

Leslie Ee—that's better ... no place like home is there? You'll find it nice and warm in here... I leave that gas fire on you see ... on a low light ... and it's surprising how the heat spreads.

Sit down ... go on ... take the weight off... I'll get that kettle on ... make us a brew.

My hands—look ... like bloody ice. Poor circulation you see ... when you're knocking on a bit. Mind you—I'm not that bloody old ... but when you get past forty-five I think you notice the difference.

No—go on—you sit yourself down... I'll tell you what—it's nice to have a bit o' company to tell the truth ... honest—you get stuck here on your own—and—well—I wouldn't say this to anybody else—but you start talking to yourself—you do! I bet folk pass this house and say, "he's going funny in there—talkin' to his bloody self"! (*He laughs*) I'll bet they do.

He removes his overcoat and scarf

Now ... just let me get me coat off ... oh, I am glad I bumped into you—I mean—it's nice to see old friends isn't it?

I've had this coat—oh, must be twenty years—and look at that—good as new. Mind you—I look after me things but that's Burton's that is ... you know—when Burton's was Burton's and you could get a suit for thirty shillings ... not like now, eh? I was there a week last Friday as a matter of fact ... thought I'd treat meself to a new jacket—you know—for work that's all—and talk about dear ... dear! ... very dear ... in fact I said to the chap—smart—tallish—only a bit of a kid actually—I said, "Are these prices right?", I said—only I didn't have me glasses and I thought I was seeing things and he said, "That's right,sir", he said—"forty-nine ninety", he said. Forty-nine ninety! I mean—fifty quid for a jacket! You'd have said they were mad years ago wouldn't you?

He hangs his coat up

(*Rubbing his hands*) Ee, that's better—you can feel that fire now can't you?

That was me mam—look. Lovely photo isn't it? I think the frame must be silver... I keep it nice and polished. I treasure that photo ... you'd never believe it but it's the only one I have... I know! Some folk have albums full of old photos don't they? ... but—well—we've never been a family for having our pictures took... I mean—we were very close—don't get me wrong—we were very close at one time—but you know what it's like...

Are you cosy? I'll get that kettle on in a minute ... you'll have a biscuit I expect ... oh, it's lovely to have a bit o' company. You know—I sit here some weekends and I never see a living soul—I don't—without a word of a lie. Thank God I've got work, eh? You'd go blummin' mad otherwise ... sitting here like one o' Piffy's with nobody to talk to...

Yes, I'm still at Cawley and Cunliffe's ... in the office like ... with Sylvia Bickerstaff. She hasn't changed ... miserable as ever... Jack left her you know—she never got over it. You remember Olive Green? Dark woman—on the stoutish side—walks with a bit of a limp? Well, he went off with her ... just like that! I mean—you never know do you. Apparently he'd been seeing her—on and off—for nigh on twelve years—or so I'm told. Mind you—I say nowt—just keep me mouth shut. I'm not a one for gossip are you?

He sits in his armchair

Mind you—I wasn't surprised ... she can be very depressing can Sylvia when she's a mind...

Silence: he looks about him: up at the ceiling

I keep saying I'll do a bit of decorating but I don't... I keep saying I'll get a tin of Dulux in Tentilow's and give this a going over ... but it's the effort isn't it? ... and I'm not one for climbing ladders... I can get very giddy up a ladder can you?

Silence: only the clock ticks

I'm glad you like the photo ... it's my one treasured possession is that...

Silence

Actually she died on the Christmas Eve... Tuesday it was ... the Salvation Army was playing *Silent Night*—you know—in the entrance hall or whatever they call it at the hospital ... talk about theatrical ... if you put it in a play they'd say it was too much! I'd been there since about eight o'clock that morning and she died at quarter past seven that night... Christmas Eve.

Everybody was very nice ... you know—kindly ... they were very sympathetic ... especially the Sister... Sister Shaw she was called ... she had a label— you know—how they do. She was expecting actually—you know—having a baby—you could tell... I expect she's had it by now ... oh, and she was nice... "Can I get you anything?", she kept saying—but I was OK... I just didn't want to be in the way... "I'm not in the way?", I said but she said I wasn't ... she was ever so nice really.

They gave me a cup of tea and all that ... and a biscuit you know ... with currants ... and one with a bit of a lemony taste ... they offered me a meal but I said no ... to tell the truth I didn't really like the look of it... I'm sure it was very nice but I'm not a lover of fish ... well, not done like that anyway. Actually, I'm sure it was very tasty but I wasn't really hungry ... well, you're not at times like that are you?

It was nice and warm in there ... a bit too warm actually but I expect they have to keep the heating turned up for all the old people ... and after all it was December.

Pause

Actually—I was expecting our Maureen to turn up but she never.

Pause

I've had a bit of a cold just lately ... the inside of my nose is ever so sore.

You see some sights in them places don't you? ... talk about tragedy. Mind you—they can be ever so funny—old people—can't they? There was one old girl opposite... Mrs Ramsden I think she was called—yes, she was—Mrs Ramsden that's it ... talk about laugh ... she'd had one of her legs off and she looked to be a bit blind and I don't think she could hear very well either but she was ever so noisy ... you know—noisy! ... and the language ... you should have heard what she kept coming out with... "Keep your voice down, Mrs Ramsden", the Sister kept saying... "You've just had a bedpan—

what're you doing—eating them?" She was ever so sharp—the Sister ... not nasty like—but witty with it ... it was all I could do to keep a straight face... "You've got a job on here", I said—but she just smiled.

They do a marvellous job in them places... I mean the nurses an' that ... they do ... wonderful job. It was a real eye-opener for me ... you know—having to sit there all day long like that ... you can't help but notice can you? They're at it all day long you know ... coming and going ... fetching and carrying ... taking temperatures ... giving injections and that... God, it'd drive me mad!

Geriatric ward they call it... Ward E... Block Four ... sounds like a prison doesn't it? ... it was very nice though ... spotlessly clean with nice blue and white curtains round the beds—you know—they pull them when you're going to the toilet an' that ... or when you die.

When me mam was gone ... you know ... they pulled them ... to keep it private and that.

Long pause

I've not been so bad actually ... well, in meself like ... except for this cold ... it will not shift.

He produces a handkerchief

I've had it about a fortnight now—if not longer ... and I still get that pain in me legs... I think it must be sciatica ... they say it attacks the legs first don't they? Mind you—you've a job keeping warm in this house ... talk about draughts ... we're on the corner you see—the end house—the wind cuts round here like a bloody knife ... you know—when it's gusty an' that.

Pause

But I've not been so bad ... considering I'm on me own...

Was that a knock?

He listens

Our Maureen keeps saying she'll call but she doesn't.

Pause

Her husband had a bit of a seizure last Wednesday ... so I believe ... mind you—I know nowt! ... she never tells me ... he could be dead and buried for all I know—she'd never tell me.

Thank God I've got me little job—eh? That keeps me going. They're having a big clear-out there you know ... they're shifting all our lot over to Moorclose House in August ... it's to do with the cuts and all that... Harry Townsend's been made redundant... I mean—you're not safe at work these days are you?

I'll have been there thirty-three years come September ... thirty-three years, eh ... time's nothing is it?

Pause

Yes—she'd been fine up until the Monday night ... you'd never have said there was anything wrong... I mean—if I'd thought she wasn't well I'd have got the doctor in wouldn't I?

We'd had our tea on the Monday ... ribs and cabbage... I always do ribs and cabbage on a Monday ... still do as a matter of fact ... oh, and she had enjoyed it ... and it was about quarter past seven—nearly *Coronation Street*—and she said she felt tired and I said, "Well, there's nothing to sit up for", I said, "watch *Coronation Street* then get to bed", I said, "it'll be Christmas Eve tomorrow and I don't have to go to work", I said... I'd finished work on the Friday you see—being as it was Christmas—and I wasn't due back until the following Monday ... they give us a week at Christmas—especially when we're so slack and that ... well, we'd be sitting there like one o' Piffy's doing nowt ... and you know what it's like in our office ... with nothing to do ... and Sylvia's no company when she's got a mood on her ... what was I saying? ... Oh aye—*Coronation Street*... I said "Go to bed after *Coronation Street* if you're not feeling up to the mark—there's nowt to sit up for", I said.

Mind you I was tired meself... I don't know what it is but I can't sit up like I used to—not when I was younger ... you know, once that clock gets to half past nine I'm half asleep in this chair.

He blows his nose

I keep meaning to get something from Jackson's for this cold—but you don't, do you? ... you keep thinking it'll go away.

Pause

Well, it must have been about five o'clock... I woke up with a start—you know—how you do ... and I don't know what it was but I knew something was wrong ... you know how you can tell? ... something's to do I thought. Now I never wake up in the night—once my head touches that pillow I'm out like a light ... funny isn't it how you seem to know? I looked at the clock... I've got two actually—in my bedroom... I've had two ever since I can remember... I think it must be in case one stops in the night then you're sunk aren't you? ... well, I looked at the clock with the luminous face and it said twelve minutes past five ... now I knew it was fast because the one with the luminous face always is ... so I reckoned it must have been about five to five... I sat up ... bolt upright and I thought something's to do I thought... I couldn't have told you what it was but I knew it was something... "Have I left that gas on?", I thought. "Have we got an intruder?" ... I mean—they broke into May Mawson's about a month ago and took her purse from under her pillow while she was fast asleep... I mean—you're not safe in bloody bed, are you? ... Shuzanyhow—I got up and looked through the window—nothing—not a sign! ... so I thought "get back to bed you silly bugger"—but you know something told me... "No", I thought—"something's up somewhere", so I went to the toilet which is just outside my door... I'm in the back you see ... still am as a matter of fact—it hasn't felt right to move into the front yet being as she's not long since gone ... and I was just flushing the toilet when I heard her...

Pause

You know—if I see our Maureen in the street I shall cut her dead—sister or not—I shall. I know you've got to live and let live but she could have come, couldn't she...?

She's gone very Jewish now, you know... I know! I'd never have believed it either but she has. Jewish this and Jewish that... I'll tell you what—she's more Jewish than he is and he *is* Jewish! They say converts are the worst, don't they...? But Jewish or not I shall give her a right mouthful when I get her on her own—and I don't care if he's there or not!

She ignores me now... I was talking to Mrs Chatterton who does for that little cripple on Moxley Street—you know—fell on the ice during that very bad winter and has never walked since—well her ... and she said—Mrs Chatterton that is—she said, "I was talking to your Maureen on Monday and I said 'Have you been up to see your Leslie since your mother died?' and she said, 'Who?'" ... she did! ... Who! Me! ... I'll give her bloody "who" when I lay my hands on her...!

He coughs—slightly short of breath with getting so excited

I'll have to get a bottle of that expectorant stuff in Boots ... they say that's good, don't they? (*Beat*) I've got some Little Lung Healers somewhere ... me mam use to swear by them ... but God knows how long she's had 'em ... I'll bet they've gone off by now.

You've got to be very careful with medicine haven't you? ... I can remember I took some stuff for my stomach once ... it'd been in that bathroom cabinet for years I believe—and I'll tell you what—it made me a bloody sight worse than I was before I took it... I chucked it out ... talk about dangerous—I mean—I could have killed meself—in the midden it went... I said to me mam, "You want to be careful what you're taking", I said... I mean, we've a tube of ointment in that cabinet—must have been there since before the war—for warts it is... I don't know who it belongs to mind—I can't remember having warts—nor me mam ... whether our Maureen was putting it on her nose or not ... and I'll tell you what—I bet that tube of ointment would fetch thousands in an antique shop ... it would! Black it is ... and the smell! (*He laughs*) It'd remove your bloody skin let alone warts.

He blows his nose again

What was I saying?

Oh, aye—about five to five it must have been—I looked out of the back bedroom window and nothing—not a sign—so I went to the toilet and I heard her ... she was awake ... now, funny this—I did something I've never done in my life—I went and pushed her door open and I've never done that in my life... I mean—a bedroom's private isn't it? ... you don't go barging into somebody's bedroom at five to five in the morning ... well, I'm glad I did now because she was sitting there—on the bed like—and I said, "Are you all right, Mam?" ... and she said, "I don't think I'm so well, Les", and I said, "Why, what's to do—have you got a pain?", I said ... well, she said she didn't have a pain but she felt rotten ... you know—rotten—sick like ... bilious I should think although she didn't actually use that word and I said, "Can I get you anything?", I said and she said, "I'd like a little drop of whisky in some hot water".

"Whisky in hot water", I thought... "what does she want whisky in hot water for?" ... "Are you sure?", I said... "Yes", she said so I come downstairs and I put a bit of whisky in a cup and I part boil the kettle—mixed the hot water into the whisky which is something I've never done in my life—and I took it up to her ... and...

Upset now by the memory

And ... oh, it did frighten me ... when I got back she'd fallen ... you know—
on the floor an' everything... I felt dead soft but it did upset me ... to see her
lying there so helpless...

He has to stop: then after a while—cheerfully

I got a letter from our Barbara last Tuesday ... you know Barbara—my sister
who's married with four children in Australia. She often writes—now she
knows I'm on my own.

And then I've got a brother in Canada ... our Graham ... he's got three ...
two boys and a girl but he's divorced now I believe ... he's been going
through a very bad patch with his wife ... drink I believe ... but I think his
divorce has come through now ... I should think so... I know it was pending
the last time he wrote... January ... just after me mam died ... that's why he
couldn't come over see ... he said he'd have it all to go through ... solicitors
and lawyers and all that messing they have to do ... he wanted custody you
see—seeing as she was unfit because she was pissed three parts of the time...
Shocking really... I'm glad I don't have any of that anyway...

Pause

He's my favourite ... me brother... Graham.

There were five of us originally... I had another brother—Rupert—but he
died when he was two and a half ... diphtheria I think they said it was but I've
never been absolutely sure ... we never mention him.

Yes, there was me—I'm the eldest ... our Barbara in Australia—our
Graham—my favourite—he's in Canada—our Rupert—he died ... and
her... Kosher Lil—our Maureen—she's round the corner in Paxino Street
but she might as well be up the Orinoco for all I see of her...

Now, please, don't get me wrong—I've nothing against them—our milkman's
Jewish and you couldn't meet a nicer chap ... but he doesn't ram it down your
throat every time he comes to the door—not like her—and it's only her ...
her husband's as nice as anything ... he's got a funny name... Alcatraz—
something like that—I can't say it because it's foreign—but he's fine ... it's
her! And funny enough she even looks Jewish because she's always had a big
nose 'as our Maureen ... we used to call her "old big conk". (*He laughs*) And
she didn't like it. Me dad was going to pay for her to have it done when she

was fourteen but she said she was frightened of the pain... I would have thought any amount of pain was better than having a nose like that!

Pause

Mind you—it's come in useful as it turned out.

Pause

So, you see, I'm an uncle quite a few times over ... let me see—I've got two nieces and two nephews in Australia ... and one niece and two nephews in Canada—so that's ... I was never any good at sums ... four nephews and three nieces ... and if our Rupert had lived I might have had more ... you wouldn't credit it, would you? Our Maureen tried for a baby, so she says—but he had a very low sperm count apparently so they couldn't manage it. But I haven't done so bad, have I? I expect they call me Uncle Leslie ... well, they would wouldn't they? What am I talking about—they'd hardly call me Uncle Sam would they?—me name's Leslie. (*He rises—he seems lost, distracted*) I'd best get that kettle on... (*But he doesn't do anything*)

You know it's forty-five p for a cup of coffee in Aspinal's ... well, what used to be Aspinal's on the market ... it's called The Cosy Crumpet now ... something like that—I ask you—nine shillings for a cup of coffee ... you'd have said they were daft years ago wouldn't you? ... but I like a cup of coffee after I've done me shopping of a Friday dinnertime... I take an extended dinner-hour on a Friday—whip round the shops—I always know what I want see—I'm not a fancy eater ... well, me mother wasn't either—so I always know what I'm buying—then I cross over the road at Boots—get me veg at Myra's stall on the market then have a coffee and two slices of toast in Aspinal's ... saves me bothering ... in fact that's where I met George Jessup last week ... you know George—Jessup—skens a bit and talks with a stammer ... lovely man though ... his life's been no picnic—married to what's-she-called ... wheels her around in a chair ... it started in her legs see—now it's crept all the way up and she's a very big Jehovah's Witness ... so it doesn't do you any good—see.

At least me Mam didn't have all that so we can count ourselves lucky, can't we?

Pause

It's funny when you look back on your life isn't it? ... you wonder what it's all been for... I mean—it must be different if you've made a name for yourself ... or if you've had a family ... that must be nice I suppose because at least you know there's somebody who'll remember you... I'm not saying I won't be remembered—I'm not saying that at all... I've got me nieces and nephews haven't I? ... but I do miss me mam... I'm not being morbid—I wouldn't do that—but—well, you can't live with somebody all your life and not miss them can you? I never married you see... I don't think I would have actually—but you can never tell...

Pause

Well—I gave her the whisky in hot water and I picked her up... I'll tell you what—there wasn't much of her but she was one hell of a weight ... shuzanyhow—I got her down here actually... I thought well she'll be better off in front of the fire I thought—or on the sofa ... now, she wasn't so bad once she was downstairs—she seemed to perk up a bit so there was no need to panic ... and to tell the truth she nodded off... I suppose it must have been about twenty to six by now and I thought—well she'll sleep it off I thought— you know—the way you do ... and the funny thing was—I wasn't worried... I mean—I'd have called the doctor right away if I'd been worried but I wasn't so I didn't ... and where do you get a doctor at that time of the morning? ... I'd have had to knock Hilda up because we're not on the telephone ... honest—the times I've thought about it but you don't do you? ... Anyway— as dawn broke over Mrs Tyson's she began to wake up a bit... and I said, "Are you feeling any better?", I said ... she looked a bit dazed... "How're you feeling?", I said...

And that's when she said it...

He blows his nose

I'll have to get something for this cold ... it's no use—it's all behind me eyes—look—I'm not crying—it's this bloody cold.

Pause

I could do with getting away actually—you know—a short break... I mean— I can please meself now—I'm not restricted... I could go to Australia if I fancied ... or Canada ... they've begged me to go ... but it's the getting there isn't it? Planes. I'm not a lover of air travel... I've never been in one mind— but I can imagine ... I'd be ill. (*He laughs*) Actually—you'll never believe this—but I've never been out of this country ... no—tell a lie—I've been to Wales ... once—when I was seventeen I went to Wales with...

The memory, an unpleasant one, prevents him telling us the name

Rhyl it was ... at least I think it was Rhyl... Prestatyn? ... summat like that...
I wasn't struck ... and there's nothing like your own bed is there? ... I mean—
I don't mind going anywhere but I'm glad when I'm back ... no place like
home is there?

Pause: still haunted by that day with his mother

Yes—she woke up a bit and I said, "Are you feeling any better?" ... and that's
when she said it ... just like that ... oh, it did strike home ... my stomach
turned over... "I'm dying, Les", she said... "I'm dying"... "Don't talk so
daft", I said—"You're no more dying than I am", I said ... but she said it
again—"I'm dying", she said...

Well—"that's it", I thought—I thought I'm not sitting here like one of
Piffy's—I've got to do something ... now, I looked at the clock on the
mantelpiece and it said ten past seven so it'll show you how long she'd been
asleep ... now, that clock can be slow so I looked at this one here and it said
twenty-five past so I reckoned it must have been about twenty past seven...
"I'm getting the doctor", I said—I knew she wouldn't like it but I'd had
enough... "Look", I said, "you're not so well so I'm going across to Hilda's
to phone the doctor", I said—but I don't honestly think she heard me ... she
was half asleep ... well, to tell the truth she looked to be in a bit of a daze—
and if I'm honest with meself I knew then that it was serious whatever it was
... but she *looked* OK... I mean—all right—I suppose she might have been
a bit of a funny colour but she *looked* all right—really—so I can't blame
myself can I? I know *she* thinks it's all my fault for not getting the doctor
sooner but it's all right for *her* to talk ... she wasn't here was she? ... too busy
being bloody Jewish!

He calms himself

Well, Hilda phoned the doctor and I'm not kidding—he was here inside ten
minutes so I've no complaints there... Doctor Hempling—German I believe
but you'd never know ... fag stuck in his mouth—makes you wonder doesn't
it—I mean—there they are telling us not to smoke and there's him with a fag
stuck in his gob...

"Let's have a look at you, Mrs Latchmore", he said... "How old is she?", he
said and I said, "Seventy-nine", and he said, "Oh", he said—just like that ...
and then he used a word I've not heard in yonks—he said, "I think she's
moribund".

I mean—I think I knew what he meant but it's a very biblical word that, isn't it? ... Moribund ... very biblical word I thought.

"She'll have to go in right away", he said, "but you'll be lucky if she makes the ambulance", he said... "she's definitely moribund".

Pause

Well, I couldn't think straight—I didn't know what to do did I—it was all happening so quick ... moribund I thought... Hilda came across... "Whatever's to do?", she said... "She's moribund", I said—"Oh, my God!", she said, "there's always something at Christmas", she said but I'd no idea what she was talking about—I mean we've always been all right at Christmas haven't we?

Now—without a word of a lie—and don't ask me how—that ambulance was here—outside that front door—within quarter of an hour so you can't complain there can you? ... I mean—I've heard such tales about three hours and more but without a word of a lie that ambulance was here inside fifteen minutes—talk about quick!

Oh and they were nice—the ambulance men—two there were—cheerful—smiling—and ever so helpful. "Come on, missis, we're taking you on your holidays", one of 'em said ... could only have been in his twenties—smart—tallish ... the other one was more my age—balding on top... "Now, don't worry, Sir", they said to me, "just get your hat and coat—I'm sure you'll want to come with us". She looked up at them—you know—the way she does...

She seemed to know something was going on but she didn't seem to mind... I think she knew really—I mean, she'd never been in an ambulance in her life. I'll tell you what—it was my first time too... I've always dreaded it but there's nothing to it... I just sat there and held her hand—you know—how you do. "Can I have a drink?", she kept saying but I was helpless wasn't I? ... "You can have a drink when we get there", I said... I was dying of thirst meself to tell the truth—I mean—I'd been up since five to five ... then she said, "Where are we going?" ... well, what d'you say? ... I said, "Don't worry, love—we'll soon be there"...

Pause

Actually ... funny this... I thought about our Judy ... well, you'll not remember but me grandma had a dog... Judy it was called ... never left the house—didn't know what a walk was ... stayed in all the time ... just went into the back yard to do its business and that ... well, I had to take her to be destroyed ... you know—at the RSPCA in Henrietta Street ... could have only been about eleven—me that is—not the dog—the dog was at least a hundred I should think ... talk about old—she couldn't see proper—and she was deaf—I used to call her... "Judy", I used to say ... not a sign! She couldn't hear me you see ... and me grandma said, "Les", she said, "if I give you sixpence will you take our Judy to the destructor—I'll give you sixpence", she said ... well, I mean, sixpence was a lot of money in them days ... just after the war it was...

Time's nothing is it?

Shuzanyhow—we tied a bit of string round her neck—she'd never had a lead seeing as she'd never been outside that door see ... and I had to drag her for miles... I mean, it was miles to Henrietta Street ... still is ... and she knew where she was going see... "First time they've taken me out", she must have thought, "and they're taking me to the destructor—what a bloody life!"

It's funny—but I was reminded of her when I was in that ambulance...

Long pause

They all die, don't they? Sooner or later. Jessie Cosgrove dropped dead in Fitton's I believe ... just like that ... one minute buying a quarter of boiled ham—the next—rigid on the floor ... you never know do you? And Elsie Taylor—school teacher—they buried her a week last Wednesday ... she was dead. Joyce tells me all this—she knows all the ins and outs ... who's dead—who's had a baby—who's in clink ... she's a nosey bugger but she means no harm ... it's how she passes the time.

He blows his nose again

This hanky's wet through—look.

Pause

Was that a knock?

Pause

Yes—so I sat there all day with her... I held her hand ... she'd wake up for a minute ... then she'd drop off again ... they'd given her one of them drip things—you know—in her arm an' that ... but nothing else—no injections or owt like that—I suppose they knew it was pointless...

Actually—you'd have thought I'd been bored—but I wasn't ... there was too much going on ... they were even putting up decorations—in the ward like—for Christmas an' that... I don't know why because nobody was looking at them but I expect they have to make the effort, don't they? Then it was coffee-time ... then dinner-time ... then afternoon visitors. (*He laughs*) The noisy woman had her daughter arrive... Eva ... that's what she was called—Eva ... and I'll tell you what—the old girl was even shouting at her!

"Where the ballsing hell have you been?", she said. Honestly—she knew more words than me and I'm a man! "I'm friggin' dying here", she shouted—she did. Everybody turned to look the other way—you know, the way you do when you're ashamed ... the daughter said, "Shh, Mam, keep your voice modulated", she said. You could see she was very embarrassed ... her face was flushed with it.

I tell you—you see some sights in them places. I'd hate to go like that—wouldn't you? Making a fool of meself. It's the daughter I felt sorry for—you know—Eva ... she looked to be ever so nice ... nice hair she had ... a bit old-fashioned but—you know—nice ... bit of a school teacher I should fancy but I didn't ask ... she was a "Miss" at any rate because I heard Sister Shaw call her "Miss Ramsden"... "Don't worry, Miss Ramsden", she said, "we have it all day long in here—she shouts from breakfast-time to supper!", she said ... she didn't mean it nasty-like—she was trying to comfort her that's all...

Pause

You'll have a cup of tea with me in a minute won't you? ... I usually brew up at about this time ... it's routine... I like to stick to routine, don't you?

Pause

It's funny but I've gone right off chips—have you?

I used to be a very big chip eater—but now—well, I can take 'em or leave 'em. I'm quite content with a boiled potato—or sometimes I do a bit of mash for a change ... plenty of butter—a drop of milk—lots of pepper and salt...

I quite enjoy that...

He stares out into middle distance: lost

Then—at about twenty past four a funny thing happened ... who should come into the ward but Councillor Taylor ... you know—Lady Harriet Taylor ... she's very big on the Council—a Justice of the Peace and all that—well her ... apparently, so Sister Shaw said later, she always comes round on Christmas Eve—you know—to wish everybody a merry Christmas ... elegant woman—very smart—big bust—husband died when they were on holiday in Portugal—they had to fly him back—well her... "Mr Latchmore", she said—you know—as if she'd known me all her life—"What a very sad Christmas it is for you", she said. Oh, she was nice ... she had that fur coat on ... and a beautiful hat in royal blue with a feather ... she knows how to dress... "Mr Latchmore", she said... I stood up—you know—how you do ... it wasn't necessary because she has absolutely no side to her at all but I've always thought you lose nothing by being polite... "Now, don't get up", she said—but I did... "How's your poor old mother?", she enquired... "She's not so well", I said, "but they haven't said what's to do with her" ... she smiled—she's got beautiful teeth for a woman her age... "We'll pray for a miracle", she said, "won't we Miss Butterworth?" ... she had her friend with her—Miss Butterworth... "You know my companion", she said, "Dorothy Butterworth?" ... well, I did but I just smiled ... actually, Sylvia in our office says they're lesbians but you know Sylvia—she can be very bad-minded... "God bless you, Mr Latchmore", she said as she went away.

"I'll bet she's no knickers on under that fur coat!", shouted Mrs Ramsden ... we were all terribly embarrassed...

Pause

Actually—it was just after Lady Harriet had gone that me mam woke up ... she opened her eyes—you know—and looked about her...

"Is it nearly over?", she said ... well, I didn't know what to say did I? ... "Is it nearly over?" ... I thought she meant—well, you know ... then she said, "Are you a doctor?" ... "No", I said, "I'm Les—I'm Leslie", I said... "I'm sitting here" ... she looked about her again—I could tell she wasn't sure where she was... "You've just missed Lady Harriet", I said... "Lady Harriet Taylor came to have a look at you and you were asleep", I said ... then she said a funny thing ... she said, "Are we going home?", and I said, "Soon"... "We'll go home soon", I said... "Which way are we going?", she said... "We'll catch the 59 bus and go that way", I said ... and then—it's funny when you come to think—she said—"I think I'll go a different way tonight", and I said, "Well, you can please yourself can't you?", I said...

Funny that, wasn't it? I suppose she must have been wandering in her sleep...

Then she said, "Can I have a drink?" ... well, I lifted her head and I gave her some water ... out of one of them little cups with a spout... "Here", I said, "drink this" ... and she did ... she looked so helpless...

But she wasn't in pain ... that doctor said afterwards—"She wasn't in pain, Mr Latchmore"...

Well, I gave her a drink and then she just smiled at me and said, "Will you tell our Les"...

"I *am* Les", I said but she was asleep again ... then I think *I* must have dozed off—I must have done because when I looked at me watch it was ten to six... I'd been sitting there for the best part of ten hours... I mean I'd been there since before eight that morning, hadn't I? ... so that's nearly ten hours isn't it?...

And then it happened.

Another Sister came over to me ... not Sister Shaw this time... "I think you should make a move", she said, "your mother could last till the morning and you're looking very tired, Mr Latchmore", she said. "Where's Sister Shaw?", I said... "Oh, Sister Shaw's gone home long since", she said, "we don't work for ever you know—she's gone home to her husband—she's not on again till Boxing Day"...

She was very nice ... don't get me wrong—I'm not saying she wasn't nice— but she had a different manner to Sister Shaw ... a bit sharper perhaps but then I dare say they have to be—eh? ... but she wasn't as friendly in a way...

"D'you think I should go then?", I asked...

"Well, I'm not telling you to go", she said, "but I think I should say in all fairness that your mother could see the night through and you are looking very, very tired—why not nip home now and have a bit of a lie down—we'll ring you if anything happens, Mr Latchmore"...

"But we're not on the phone", I said... "How will I know?" ... "What about relatives—can we contact a relative?", she said...

Now, I was about to tell her that I had a sister in Paxino Street ... but something told me not to—so I gave her Hilda's number... "That's my neighbour across the road", I said, "she's very good—she'll always take a message", I said...

"Well, if you don't mind me saying—that seems the wisest thing to do under the circumstances", she said...

Silence

It's all my fault... I'm too soft... I should have insisted on staying shouldn't I? ... I mean—I didn't want to be in the way—I didn't want to be under their feet and all that—but I wasn't really—was I? ... I mean—I was just sitting there holding her hand wasn't I? ... but you're not sure of your rights are you? ... and I didn't want to cause a fuss or anything... I mean—I didn't want to get anybody into trouble you see—you understand—don't you?...

Pause

"How will you get home?", the new Sister said... "Are you mobile, Mr Latchmore?"...

"How d'you mean—mobile?", I said... "Have you got a car?", she said... "No", I said and she said, "What will you do—catch the 59?" ... "Yes", I said ... and she just stood there—looking down at me—I mean you'd have thought she'd have busied herself a bit ... to give me a couple of minutes to think about it—but she just stood there—slightly impatient, like—as if I had to make me mind up there and then...

I looked up at her... "I'd best go then", I said... "I think it's the best thing—after all we don't want you poorly, do we?", she said...

I looked down at me mam ... she was fast asleep... "Will she be all right?", I said...

"She'll be fine—we'll look after her", she said...

So I went.

I put me hat and coat on and I went.

He is upset—crying softly

And I stood at the bus stop ... and when it came... I had no money... I'd been so rushed that morning I'd come out without any money... I said to the driver, "I've no money", I said ... he looked at me a bit funny... "We're not a sodding charity", he said ... and I just cried—I couldn't help meself ... on that bus—I just cried... I was upset you see...

I'll pop that kettle on in a minute... I'm sorry.

Silence—he pulls himself together—blows his nose—then, almost with a laugh

You must think I'm daft ... telling you all this ... but it's the first time I've told anybody, you see... I'm a soft bugger, aren't I?...

Well, there was this woman—on the bus—oh, she was nice... "I'll pay for him", she said... "Where're you going to, love?"

"I'm going home", I said... "Thirty-three p", I said, "top of Grimshaw Lane—by the Catholic church", I said... "If you give me your address I'll send it to you"... But she said it didn't matter... "It's Christmas, love", she said, "have it on me" ... wasn't that nice of her...?

Pause

People can be nice—can't they?

Pause

Well, I got off the bus at the top of our street ... the driver gave me a funny look—you know how they do... I felt like saying something but I kept my mouth shut ... just you wait, I thought—just you wait till your mother's dying, I thought...

I walked up our street ... and it's a funny thing but there was no light on in our house ... well, there was nobody there was there? ... but that was the first time in my life that I'd come home and the light wasn't on ... funny that isn't it? ... me mam was always here you see ... sitting here waiting for me...

Well, I'd just put the key in the door when Hilda shouted across... "Les", she shouted... "they've just been on the phone", she said, "the hospital—they've just rung up—you've got to go back—your mam—she's taken a turn for the worse—you've got to go back"...

"But I've just come back from there", I said... "They sent me home", I said...

"they said she'd see the night through" … me stomach was churning over—you know how it does… "What shall I do?", I said… "Come on—Jack'll run you up in the car", she said… "You can't go on the 59—it'll take all night"…

Silence

Jack was very good.

He ran me back to the hospital.

But it was too late.

I knew that… I knew it was too late…

Silence: the clock ticks on

You can hear that wind, can't you? … it cuts round that corner like a knife…

The Salvation Army was playing *Silent Night* when I got back … in the entrance hall or whatever they call it…

I knew as soon as I got into the ward that she'd gone … they'd drawn the blue and white curtains round her bed … the Sister was ever so nice really… "I'm very sorry", she said… "Why not go into my little office and we'll get you a cup of tea and a biscuit?" … but I didn't fancy it…

"What happened?", I said…

"Just after you left she woke up", she said… "We could see it was nearly over—we did all we could, Mr Latchmore…"

"Did she wonder where I'd gone?"

"No—I'm sure she didn't", she said.

"Did she say anything?", I asked.

"Well, she just looked at me and smiled, Mr Latchmore".

Pause

"She just smiled—and she called me Maureen … she must have thought I was Maureen…"

Pause

"Who's Maureen?", she asked.

Pause

"Me sister", I said… "Maureen's me sister".

Pause

"She lives on Paxino Street…"

Wind softly at a distance: the clock

Slow fade

ACT II

Lights come up on Leslie's living-room

Maureen is standing by the window, lace curtain pulled aside, looking out into the street

After a while, she leaves the window and comes to stand by Leslie's armchair

Maureen I thought I heard a car—but it's nothing. Time hangs heavy when you're waiting, doesn't it…?

Honestly, I've had my eye on that clock since half past nine this morning.

She takes a small handkerchief from the sleeve of her cardigan and wipes her nose

The post was late again—did you notice? Quarter past ten this time. Still—everything's falling apart, isn't it?

I mean, he's a nice enough chap, don't get me wrong—but have you ever seen him sober? I don't like having to complain but I do think somebody should write to the Post Office—I do.

Not that they'd take a blind bit of notice, I'm sure, but I don't think it does any harm to have a bit of a moan occasionally. Keeps people on their toes as my husband is always saying. He's a stickler for correctitude—he is. Everything on time and strictly to the letter and it's done him no harm, has it? He wouldn't have got where he's got if he'd been slap-happy.

(*Looking about her*) I did run round with that Hoover but you'd never know it. I think it's buggered.

She consults her little wrist watch

Do you make it ten to or am I a bit fast…? (*She checks with one of the clocks*) 'Course, the trouble with this house is every clock tells a different story. It can be twenty to in that kitchen and twenty past in here. I suppose it's still last Easter Monday in his bedroom.

She sits

I'd better just take the weight off. In case there's a lot of standing later. (*Beat*) This is usually when I have a cigarette—but I've given up. It's not knowing what to do with your hands, though, isn't it? I have tried knitting but you run out of things to knit, don't you? And who'll wear a home-made pullover these days? My husband wants the latest designs from Marks now. (*Beat: looking down at her feet*) Nineteen ninety-nine on the market these shoes and they're ever so comfortable. Japanese the woman said but you'd never know, would you?

I'm a devil for shoes—I am. I'll buy shoes just to pass the time me, you know. My husband's forever saying "You've not been buying more shoes, have you?", he is. (*She laughs*) He goes mad. "You've a wardrobe full of shoes", he says. "They'll be calling you Matilda Markos!", he says. Talk about laugh…

Suddenly she shivers slightly

Now did you see that? I wouldn't mind if I could get warm. The coldest house in history is this. Always was. Even when we were kids.

Honestly, the times I used to say to Mam, "Mam", I said, "get some radiators installed—splash out a bit". But would she take any notice? I mean, if you can't be warm at home where can you be warm…?

It's like not being on the telephone, you see. She could be very stubborn when she wanted. Like him. Our Leslie. "You might as well be marooned on a desert island", I said. Talk about living in the past. He didn't get her a coloured television till nineteen eighty-nine, you know. She was stuck with that old black-and-white thing … the picture all fuzzy and lob-sided. Frightened to death of spending money, you see. She watched the snooker for years without knowing all the balls were a different colour! She never knew there was a Channel Four till she pressed the wrong button by mistake.

But he's always been tight with money has our Les. "You're as mean as a butcher's dog!", I used to say when we were kids. But you know our Leslie— "We're all right—leave us alone—we're happy as we are".

I did offer to buy them a microwave but he turned it down. "They're very handy", I said but he wouldn't listen. He'd have probably ended up trying to wash his socks in it. I tell you—if people only knew the half of it.

I mean—it's like this place—just look at it. Talk about a mess. It hasn't had a lick of paint since they buried Winston Churchill. And the junk. There's a pile of newspapers in that kitchen dating back to nineteen forty-five—there is. And half these ornaments I wouldn't give house-room.

Mind you—I've got my eye on them pot dogs—fetch a fortune now in Cartwright's they would.

She'd never throw anything away, me mam, you know. There's a sixteen-piece bone china tea service and a mock crystal sherry decanter in that sideboard and have they ever been used...? Talk about hoarding—I'll bet there's folk who'd pay good money just to come and have a good gawp at this lot—they could sell tickets—they could!

I mean, you've got to move with the times in this day and age, haven't you? Oh, I've had to bite my tongue some an' often I can tell you—people don't know the half of it.

She wipes her nose again

Oh, you know, I couldn't half murder a Silk Cut Extra Mild now. You get very twitchy, don't you? (*Beat*) I'd make us a brew but there's no sign of a tea-bag out there. And he's had that jar of Nescaff since Adam was a lad. I mean, we're not very big coffee-drinkers—my husband's got this thing about too many stimulants—but I've always got a fresh jar in in case we fancy a bit of a change.

She adjusts her bra-strap under her blouse

We often have a small glass of Harvey's Bristol Cream in the evenings now, you know. Just the one—we'd never overdo it. It goes down very nicely with the nine o'clock news.

From a pocket she produces a packet of Polo mints and pops one into her mouth

I suck on these but they'd drive you mad in the finish. And I'm covered in those Nicorette patches. My husband thought they were plasters. "You look as if you've been trying to commit suicide", he said. But it's all right for him—he's no idea what it's like because he's never smoked, you see.

And now he's always on about passive smoking—honestly, you don't stand a chance, do you?

I can remember when we all smoked, can you? There was no harm in it then, was there? I had a great uncle who smoked eighty a day, you know. Lived till he was ninety-one and got run over by a bus. I mean—you never know, do you? (*Beat*) I can't even offer you a biscuit because there's nothing in his cupboards. There's half a packet of almond slices but I wouldn't risk it. Honestly, it's no way to live, is it? Living from hand-to-mouth like that—just buying what you need for the day and being shown up when unexpected visitors call round to see you.

She rises and wanders about the room: she seems slightly on edge, nervous perhaps, uneasy: she inspects the things on the sideboard

Have you tried those apricot sponge surprises in Marks? You do pay a little bit extra but they only use the finest ingredients so you're on to a winner anyway.

(*Finding a small pile of cards*) Last year's Christmas cards—look. "Across the miles at Christmas" … oh, it's from our Barbara in Australia. (*Throwing the cards into a waste paper basket*) More than I ever get.

I've stopped sending cards to her anyway. And our Graham in Canada. I used to pop in a bit of something for the kids but I never got a thank you—kiss-me-arse—nothing! Mind you, I was never given our Graham's new address and I know our Les had it.

It doesn't bother me. I never got on that well with them even before they went abroad … well, not since…

She leaves it unsaid

Families, eh—you're better off without them—I mean, you can choose your friends, can't you—but not your family.

She pulls aside the curtain again and peers out

The state of these windows—look. There's Joyce-next-door (*she waves*) doing her garden and pretending she hasn't seen me…

She doesn't speak to me now, you know. I was trying to tidy up that back yard the day before yesterday and she was just pegging her washing out. All I said was, "It's still nippy without a cardigan", and she just ignored me. She did. Oh, please yourself, I thought—it's no skin off my nose.

Then there's Hilda across the road. She's gone all snooty.

She leaves the window and comes back into the room

You'd think all this was my fault, wouldn't you? They think I've been neglectful but I've always done what I could if I was *asked*—you know me— I'll lend a helping hand to anybody *if* I'm *asked*—but you've got to be *asked*, haven't you? Otherwise people just think you're poking your nose in.

"You worry too much, Maureen", my husband's always saying. "They'll *ask* if they want anything". But he doesn't understand, you see—it's different for him. He's got no family. Well, he's got his mother and his twin sister but they're still in Poland and I expect things are different over there…

She sits again—trying hard to keep calm

I've left him a hotpot in the oven so he's only to switch it on. He would have come today but since his stroke he finds it difficult to stay awake—and standing about crucifies him. You see, people don't know the half—I've got it all to do for him, haven't I?

So I've nothing to feel guilty about, have I? You know me mam and our Leslie never turned up at my wedding, do you? And that wasn't me mam—it was our Les.

Pretended he'd lost the invitation and didn't know where the synagogue was.

"Miles Platting", he said. "We don't even know where Miles Platting is … how can you expect me mam to get to Miles Platting?"

I mean, this is Miles Platting we're talking about—not Hong Kong…!

Oh no. I knew what it was all about. My poor husband knew what it was all about. They couldn't accept that I was marrying into another faith. All our Leslie could say was, "What will Father O'Fee say?"

"Father O'Fee", I said. "What's it got to do with Father O'Fee? We haven't invited Father O'Fee", I said.

"What will we have to do?", he kept saying.

"What d'you mean—what will you have to do?", I said. "Just stand there and watch us get married", I said.

"There won't be any funny business, will there?", he said. "Mam's in no fit state to be grovelling about", he said.

"Grovelling about!", I said. "It's a wedding", I said, "nobody's expecting you to scrub the floors!"

"Well, I don't know what they get up to", he said. "They're different to us, aren't they?"

He was frightened, you see. Afraid of something he didn't understand— that's the top and bottom of it. That's how we were brought up in this house. Suspicious of everything. Anything odd—anything strange or "foreign" we either ignored or made fun of it—we did! The first time we ever saw a black man, me grand-dad nearly set the dog on him!

And all that rubbish about Father O'Fee—well, we know what all that was about, don't we? Just because I was changing my religion we were devout Catholics all of a sudden. Now, I know me dad went to Mass every Sunday— every Sunday regular as clockwork he went to Mass—but me mam would never have anything to do with it—nor would we. I mean, we went to Dorothy Street Juniors, didn't we? Dorothy Street Juniors then on to Moorclose Secondary. If we were that Catholic why weren't we sent to Our Lady of the Immaculate Conception or whatever they called it on Derrydale Street—tell me that!

Beat: as if to calm herself, she pops another Polo mint into her mouth

Poor Dad. Not one of us ever asked him why he went to church. I don't suppose he knew himself why he went. Terrified not to I expect—frightened of Father O'Fee I shouldn't wonder. 'Course Mam never trusted the Pope because he was a foreigner, you see. In fact, she once burned Dad's picture of him just for coming home drunk! "At least Jesus was English!", she said.

What a life, eh...?

There's a name for it all my husband says... "xenophobia" they call it. I looked it up in the dictionary—"an intense dislike of foreigners", it said. Well, that's my family all over—xenophobic in the extreme. And our Leslie the worst of the lot.

You know he wouldn't go near a pizza, do you? Indian food—Chinese—Italian—he'd run a mile. One whiff of garlic and he'd come over all bilious.

And yet he'd eat tripe. Tripe! Boiled and soaked in vinegar. Cow heel, ribs and cabbage or that nasty brown stuff they get from sheep. Now, I ask you, who in their right mind would eat all that!

Small-minded—that just about sums our Leslie up.

Her hands are twitching—her nerves on edge

Oh, bugger it—I'm having a cigarette!

She spits out her Polo into her handkerchief, goes to her handbag, takes out a packet of Silk Cut cigarettes and lights one

It's no use persecuting yourself, is it? I mean, what else have I got in life? And who's to say you can't be poisoned by Polos?

She searches the room for an ashtray: unable to find one she goes to the sideboard, brings out a saucer

Oh, sod it—she'll never know now.

She takes a deep drag on the cigarette and sighs with relief

Oh, it's like nectar, isn't it? I mean, if you can't have a fag what can you have? A fag, a pot of tea, your feet up on the pouffe and the world's your oyster, isn't it?

She takes another drag

I always think of *Seven Brides for Seven Brothers* at times like this, I do. (*She smiles to herself*) I had my very first fag watching *Seven Brides for Seven Brothers* with Jane Powell and Howard Keel in Technicolour at the old Essoldo on Middleton Road. Hilda, Joyce and me—sitting in the back row—sneaking a sly drag on a Woodbine given to us by Charlie Shorrocks. "Go on", he said, "treat yourselves—live a little". He fancied both Hilda and Joyce, you know. He didn't fancy me, though. Nobody fancied me. I think Joyce let him touch her knickers—you know—in exchange for the Woodbine. I was too busy having a sly drag and enjoying the film.

Happy days, eh. I used to go out with Hilda and Joyce all the time when we were teenagers, you know. Dancing on Wednesdays at the Co-op Hall—I only used to watch—I was never much good at dancing—the pictures twice a week—the Essoldo on Thursdays and the Rialto at the weekend. Oh, and we did used to laugh. They'd discovered sex by then and were always trying to pick up lads. I just tagged along not really understanding what it was all about.

Mind you, nothing ever happened. Things were different in them days. I used to watch them—being groped in the graveyard on our way home. It never appealed to me. All that fumbling and giggling. I was happy with a packet of crisps and a bag of humbugs.

Her smile fades—she flicks ash on to the saucer held in her other hand

But they've forgotten all that now, haven't they. Won't even speak to me now. Well, sod 'em. If they want to be funny, I can be funny.

And I know who's at the bottom of it—it's not Hilda—Hilda wouldn't say boo to a goose—it's her—next-door-Joyce—Miss Bossy-Kecs! And we know why, don't we? She's jealous of me and my husband because we're happy and she's not. Well, whose fault's that?

She should never have married Cyril—we all knew that. I mean, don't get me wrong, he's a nice enough chap but ... well, he's not all there, is he? And he's certainly not all there (*lowering her voice*) in the men's department—if you know what I mean—and I know it's true because it was Joyce herself who told me ... in confidence ... which is why I've never told anyone else.

She takes a satisfying drag on her cigarette

They've never... (*she tries to indicate with signs*) never ... well, you know. Consummated themselves. Apparently—they tried it once on their wedding night—but he got his head stuck in the bed railings. I know! It must have been awful for her. There she was—trapped underneath him—pinned to the mattress—calling for help—but nobody came. Well, her mother was deaf, you see. Shocking really. It had such a profound effect on him—they've never tried it since. Shame, isn't it?

Oh, she forgets I know all this. I expect she thinks I've forgotten ... well, I haven't.

Oh, I know what you're thinking—what about their Doreen. Well, she's not Cyril's child—that much I do know. You know Ted Orme? Oh, you do—that little butcher on the corner of Albatross Street—stammers and walks with a bit of a limp—well him. He had a bit of a thing with Joyce behind his wife's back and Doreen was the result. You see—it all happens round here. And Cyril was happy because it made him look good—and Ted was very good to Joyce. She got free meat till Doreen left school and went to work.

(*About the cigarette*) Oh, I am enjoying this. It calms you down and loosens the tongue, doesn't it...?

You know I invited them to my wedding, do you? Joyce and Hilda. But they said they had something else on that day. Oh, sod you, I thought. I had four people at my wedding, did you know that? Four! And two of them were strangers who'd turned up expecting a funeral! The Rabbi was embarrassed—I was embarrassed—and my poor husband was nearly in tears. I mean, the happiest day of my life and nobody turned up. What with his family in Poland—my lot scattered to the four winds—talk about a picnic! And folk round here wonder why I get upset. Upset! It's a wonder I ever spoke to our Leslie again. Oh, no—I know what they all thought: "Oh, our Maureen'll never get married—who'd marry our Maureen—she'll stay on and look after Mam". Well, they were wrong, weren't they? One look and it was love at first sight with me and my husband and what did it matter to me if he couldn't speak proper English and he'd had one of his lungs removed and couldn't get his breath—that's not his fault, is it? "He's too old for you"—that's all our Leslie could say.

I felt like saying it's love that counts at the end of the day not jumping into bed with every fella who turns up. Oh, no, we're not supposed to mention that our Barbara *had* to get married—and we're not supposed to remember why our Graham packed his bags and fled to foreign parts—his name in all the papers. And our Leslie was no angel—what was all that about with what's-his-name in Jubilee Park? He was lucky that didn't get into *The Gazette*!

But me—me who'd never done anything wrong—me who'd led the life of a Carmelite nun almost—what credit did I get?

She smokes to calm herself down again

Still—we've shown them—haven't we?

A happy marriage—blissfully happy—we would have liked children but it wasn't to be—a beautiful home—parquet flooring—picture lights—the lot!

And them? Our Graham—on his second wife—Barbara—her husband knocks her about I believe. And as for our Leslie...

And he didn't have to stay on here with me mam—no matter what folk round here think. I know he enjoyed playing the martyr but it was his choice—nobody forced him. I mean, we always suspected he'd never get married but he could have found himself a little flat, couldn't he? I'd have kept an eye on Mam—of course I would. My husband was even willing to have her with us.

"She's your mother, Maureen", he used to say, "your mother and if anything ever happened to your Leslie she'd come and live with us". Now, wasn't that good of him—after the way he'd been treated?

And she'd have been more comfortable than she was here. I mean, we've got the new extension, haven't we? Self-contained—its own front door—toilet and washing facilities—carpet wall-to-wall. I mean, she had lino on her bedroom floor till the day she died—what sort of life's that?

She hears something outside

Was that the front gate…?

She rises to the window again

I'm sure that was the front gate. (*She looks out*) Oh, it's Mrs Tyson. Leaving flowers I expect. God, she's lost some weight, hasn't she?

Would you believe—it's coming on to rain now. That's all we need today.

She comes again to stand beside Leslie's armchair: silence: the room seems to be getting darker

(*Quieter now, reflective*) She's had no life, you know. Mrs Tyson.

There is a Mr Tyson but nobody ever sees him.

It seems they haven't spoken to each other in twenty-five years. They address one another through the furniture.

"Ask him if he wants a cup of tea", she'll say to the sideboard.

"Tell her to frig off", he replies to the fireplace.

People lead funny lives, don't they?

They have a daughter, you know. Beryl. She was in my class at school. But she went funny—you know—had a bit of a breakdown. They had to have her put away.

They never go and see her now.

We realize she is crying softly

It was Mrs Tyson who rang me, you know. Saying she hadn't seen him for a few days and did I think everything was all right.

Her anger returning—perhaps to cover her distress

You see, if he hadn't been so tight and got himself on the telephone I could have rung him, couldn't I? I could have dialled the number and said, "Is everything OK?". But as he wasn't on the phone I couldn't so I didn't.

Oh, I can guess what Joyce and Hilda have been saying … putting it about that I should have popped round sooner to check if he was all right but I wasn't his keeper, was I?

And how was I to know that he hadn't gone away for a few days? He was a free agent, wasn't he? He could come and go as he wanted. And, besides— if they were so concerned why didn't they just tap on his window to see if he was up and about?

And what about his work—obviously they didn't miss him—so whose fault is that? Oh, yes, they can send a wreath—out there on the lawn—saying "gone but not forgotten" but half of 'em in that factory didn't even know who he was!

And there's another thing—if he hadn't been feeling so well why didn't he pop round and tell me? I have got a front door, haven't I? Why didn't he knock and ask me to fetch him a doctor and you don't have to answer that because I know the answer already…

Guilt—that's what it was—guilt. All this is about guilt. He couldn't face me. I mean, staying away from my wedding's one thing—making fun of my husband's religion's another—but not letting me know my own mother had passed away…!

I had to hear it from a stranger—how do they think that made me feel? It was Lillie Crabtree from Albatross Street who told me two days after it happened! Two days! He sat all day in that hospital with her and never once thought of getting somebody to ring me—and I can never forgive him for that—never!

My mother died without even seeing me—without even mentioning my name I expect. And that's why I'm in the state I am ... that's why I've been on tablets for my nerves ever since that awful Christmas!

She has worked herself into a state

I'm sorry... I shouldn't be saying all this to you. I know you liked Leslie—but there is my side to all this. People don't know the half of it.

She wipes her face with her handkerchief

I am sorry. I'm all right now. I just wish my husband could have come. I hate funerals, don't you?

She looks at her watch again

What is the time...? Oh, look—it'll be here and I'm not ready.

She gets her coat from behind the door—it is a black coat with a black headscarf in its pocket

Getting into her coat

I hope this doesn't look too old-fashioned but it's the only black coat I have. And I didn't bother to get a hat so I'll wear this.

She puts on her headscarf then takes another handkerchief out of her pocket: if before there was even the slightest doubt, we now see Maureen is a very ordinary Lancashire woman

(*About the hanky*) I brought another—just in case.

She sits

It's funny really ... before you came I got to thinking about our Rupert...

Perhaps you'll not remember our Rupert—he was the brother I never knew. He died before I was born.

In a way I think Mam and Dad always hoped I'd make up for his loss—you know—take his place an' that. But I don't think I ever did somehow. "He was an angel", me mam used to say, "a little angel". "What did we do to have him taken from us like that?"

When I met my husband—I was happy for the first time in my life.

He never knew about Rupert.

And I never told him.

There is a ring at the front doorbell

She jumps up and runs to the window where we can see the rain falling quite heavily now

Oh, my God—that'll be him. Yes, it's here. You go on out... Tell them I'll only be a minute, eh?

Silence as she looks about the room as if for the last time. After a while, she addresses the room

Les...? Leslie—are you there, love...?

She waits for a moment as if expecting a reply

I'm sorry it had to end like this, Les. But you never made it easy for me.

And you'd only to ask—why didn't you ask...?

She gets her bag, adjusts her headscarf, and exits to the hall

We hear the front door bang

Slowly the Lights begin to fade on the empty room leaving only a pool of light around Leslie's armchair

We hear a recording of Leslie's voice saying

Leslie (*on tape*) Maureen's me sister ... she lives on Paxino Street...

Soon, the light around Leslie's chair begins to fade also

Darkness

THE END

FURNITURE AND PROPERTY LIST

Further dressing may be added at the director's discretion

ACT I

On stage: Photo of Mam in old silver frame
Armchair
2 clocks
Lace curtain on window
Sideboard. *On it*: small pile of Christmas cards
Waste paper basket

Personal: **Leslie:** overcoat, scarf, handkerchief

ACT II

Set: Saucer in sideboard
Handbag containing packet of Silk Cut cigarettes and lighter
On door hook: black coat with black headscarf and handkerchief in pocket

Personal: **Maureen**: small handkerchief, little wrist watch, packet of Polos

LIGHTING PLOT

Property fittings required: nil
1 interior. The same throughout

ACT I

To open: Overall general lighting

Cue 1   Sound of wind and clock ticking   (Page 20)
           Slowly fade lights down

ACT II

To open: Overall general lighting

Cue 2   **Maureen** stands beside **Leslie**'s armchair   (Page 30)
           Slightly fade lights down

Cue 3   **Maureen** moves to window   (Page 33)
           Rain effect outside

Cue 4   Front door bangs   (Page 33)
           Slowly fade lights to pool of light around **Leslie**'s *armchair*

Cue 5   **Leslie**: (*on tape*) ...she lives on Paxino Street...   (Page 33)
           Fade out light around **Leslie**'s *armchair*

EFFECTS PLOT

ACT I

Cue 1   **Leslie**: "…very giddy up a ladder can you?"   (Page 2)
Clock ticks in silence

Cue 2   **Leslie**: "I knew it was too late."   (Page 19)
Clock ticks on in silence

Cue 3   **Leslie**: "She lives on Paxino Street."   (Page 20)
Sound of wind softly in distance; clock ticking

ACT II

Cue 4   **Maureen**: "And I never told him."   (Page 33)
Doorbell rings

Cue 5   **Maureen** exits   (Page 33)
Presently, front door bangs

Cue 6   Light fades to pool on **Leslie**'s armchair   (Page 33)
Leslie*'s voice on tape as script page 33*